P9-CAM-466

VIEWPOINTS ON
THE
DUST BOWL

★ PART OF THE PERSPECTIVES LIBRARY ★

KRISTIN J. RUSSO

Published in the United States of America by Cherry Lake Publishing
Ann Arbor, Michigan
www.cherrylakepublishing.com

Reading Adviser: Marla Conn MS, Ed., Literacy specialist, Read-Ability, Inc.

Photo Credits: ©H. Armstrong Roberts/Getty Images, cover (left); ©George Marks/Getty Images, cover (middle); ©Dorothea Lange/Wikimedia, cover (right); ©H. Armstrong Roberts/Getty Images, 1 (left); ©George Marks/Getty Images, 1 (middle); ©Dorothea Lange/Wikimedia, 1 (right); ©H. Armstrong Roberts/Getty Images, 4; ©Everett Collection/Newscom, 7; ©Arthur Rothstein/Wikimedia, 9; ©Everett Collection/Newscom, 11; ©George E. Marsh/NOAA/Wikimedia, 12; ©Circa Images/Glasshouse Images/Newscom, 14; ©Everett Collection/Newscom, 15; ©USDA/Wikimedia, 17; ©George Marks/Getty Images, 18; ©World History Archive/Newscom, 19; ©Arthur Rothstein/Wikimedia, 20; ©akg-images/Newscom, 23; ©Kansas State Historical Society/KRT/Newscom, 24; ©Everett Collection/Newscom, 27; ©milehightraveler/Getty Images, 29; ©Dorothea Lange/Wikimedia, 32; ©Dorothea Lange/Wikimedia, 35; ©Dorothea Lange/Wikimedia, 36; ©Pictures From History/Newscom, 38; ©Library of Congress/Newscom, 43; ©Circa Images/Glasshouse Images/Newscom, 44; ©Library of Congress/MCT/Newscom, 45; ©World History Archive/Newscom, 45

491 1322

Library of Congress Cataloging-in-Publication Data has been filed and is available at catalog.loc.gov

Cherry Lake Publishing would like to acknowledge the work of The Partnership for 21st Century Learning.
Please visit *www.p21.org* for more information.

Printed in the United States of America
Corporate Graphics

TABLE OF CONTENTS

In this book, you will read about the Dust Bowl from three perspectives. Each perspective is based on real things that happened to real people who lived during the Dust Bowl. As you'll see, the same event can look different depending on one's point of view.

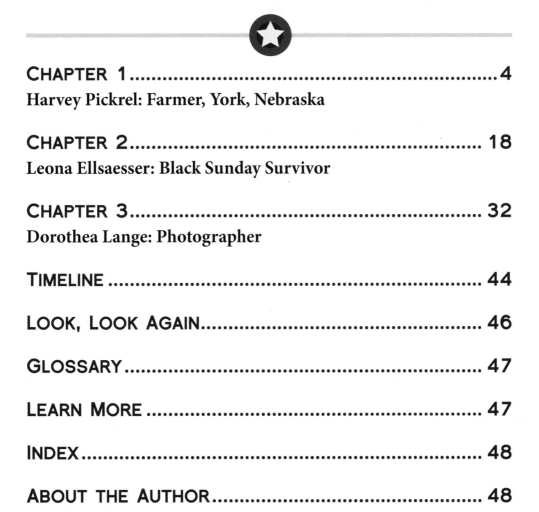

HARVEY PICKREL

FARMER, YORK, NEBRASKA

When my daddy owned the farm, now those were the good days. Sure, there was always work to be done, but we turned a **profit** and farming was a good life. My brother and I, we helped with the chores. We got up with the sun each day and fed the horses first. Then it was time to go to the cow barn and do the milking. Then the milk had to be separated to get the cream. The skim milk wasn't for us—we gave that to the pigs! All this was done before breakfast each day, and then there was plenty more to do after that.

ANALYZE THIS

Find another perspective that describes life on the Great Plains during the **Dust Bowl**. How is it similar to this perspective? How are the two different?

We harnessed the horses and headed out to the fields. The planting was done a certain way, thanks to my father's ingenuity. He'd string wires from one end of the field to the other, and every time one of those wires hit a small knob that he had placed on it, it would trip a small **mechanism** and two or three kernels of corn would drop in. He made sure the corn rows were at least 40 inches (102 centimeters) apart so there would be room for horses to get through.

Later, when I took over the farm, I had a different approach. The plow would make a deep **furrow**. But his way worked just as well. It was picking the corn that was always troublesome to me. I was not good at it. There was a special tool with a hook that was meant to make the job easier, but I struggled and always seemed to wind up spraining my wrist. It was a tough job, but of course, it had to get done. Once the corn was picked, it moved by conveyor to a sheller. When the kernels were stripped off, all you had left were the corncobs. We used those in the cook stove.

Yes, the early days were the good days, but things changed quickly. We went from horse-drawn plows to tractors, and that was a big change to get used to. The tractor didn't know that "whoa" meant stop, and sometimes you'd forget you weren't on a horse and just keep driving through the fence.

I kept on doing what I thought was right. Sometimes I'd do things the old way, and sometimes I

THINK ABOUT IT

Determine the main point of this paragraph. Pick out one piece of evidence that supports it.

PLOWING SOIL WAS CONSIDERED A NECESSARY PART OF FARMING. HOWEVER, FARMERS AFFECTED BY THE DUST BOWL PLOWED THE SOIL TOO MUCH.

found a new way. I did the best I could, but one day, the rain just stopped. The drought started in 1931, and the crops started to fail. Without grass or crops to keep the soil in place, well, it started blowing around.

★ STAYING PUT

Local newspaper editor John McCarty encouraged people to stay by forming the Last Man Club. Its pledge: "In the absence of an act of God, serious family injury, or some other emergency, I pledge to stay here . . . and . . . help other last men remain in this country." Although many farmers struggled to pay their bills and feed their families, McCarty was determined to help the suffering farmers not lose hope. By founding the Last Man Club, he urged families to stay and try to outlast the terrible weather conditions. Thanks to his efforts, three-quarters of the farmers living in the Plains states stayed.

When grasslands were plowed and crops could not grow, there were no roots to hold the fine soil in place. This resulted in devastating dust storms.

The ground was over-plowed and before too long, the dust storms came.

The dust and the dirt covered everything in their path. One day, we headed down to Great Bend, Kansas, to buy a tractor from a farmer who was giving up. He used to grow corn, he said, but the soil grew too dry, and he couldn't make a living. He sent us out to the field for the tractor, and we found it covered nearly to the top in dirt. He didn't charge us much for it, but we had to dig it out and fix it up ourselves.

We all had troubles with the dirt. "**Black Blizzards**," they called them. The man who sold me the dirt-covered tractor told us he was driving home from town one day in a dust storm so dark he missed his own driveway. Instead, he drove over his own mailbox.

I don't understand how all this happened. Our farm used to be crops and **livestock** and cattle as far as the eye could see—flat, beautiful farmland bringing us

THE SUMMER OF 1936 WAS THE MOST DIFFICULT FOR MANY FARMERS. IT WAS THE HOTTEST AND DRIEST SUMMER ON RECORD UP UNTIL THAT TIME.

beauty and sustenance, just as God promised when the pioneers fulfilled His "manifest destiny." At least that's what Daddy said. We feel abandoned now. We feel punished. What went wrong? Many families did their part generations ago when they came out here as pioneers on the Oregon Trail. Now, all we have to

ONE "BLACK BLIZZARD" TRAVELED 2,000 MILES (3,200 KILOMETERS) TO THE EAST COAST ON MAY 11, 1934. IT COVERED THE U.S. CAPITOL WITH DUST. BY COINCIDENCE, LEGISLATORS WERE INSIDE THE BUILDING AT THE TIME DEBATING A BILL ABOUT SOIL CONSERVATION.

show for decades of farming is dirt, dirt, and more dirt. If anything grows at all, the grasshoppers eat it. It's pitiful.

As a farmer, I wonder if we couldn't have seen this coming and found some way to stop it. Most of us have been farming the same land for generations. There is only so much a plot of land can take before it needs to lie fallow to heal. We didn't give our land a rest. We just kept pushing and pushing. And with the introduction of the new plows that dug deeper and deeper, we lost most of the topsoil. All we needed was a small drought to bring about trouble. What we got was about a decade of drought. In fact, we're used to getting about 20 inches (51 cm) of rainfall per year here in Nebraska. But between 1930 and 1934, rainfall dropped by so much—more than 25 percent— that we lost about 75 percent of our crop yields. Those are pretty serious numbers. No wonder all the land will give us now is dust. We pushed it to the **brink**. And no matter how good you are at planting and sowing, you can't farm without rain.

I know I'm not alone in this misery. Reports say that by 1934, about 35 million acres (14 million hectares) of old farmland can no longer grow crops, and another 125 million acres (51 million ha) is losing

DESPERATE FARMERS TRIED MANY UNORTHODOX WAYS TO MAKE IT RAIN. ONE TEXAS FARMER PAID $500 FOR A "RAINMAKER" TO FIRE ROCKETS FILLED WITH DYNAMITE AND NITROGLYCERINE TO MAKE IT RAIN. THESE STRATEGIES DID NOT WORK.

IN NEW JERSEY AND MANY OTHER STATES, VILLAGES
WITH RAMSHACKLE SHACKS CALLED "SHANTY TOWNS"
SPRUNG UP, PROVIDING THE ONLY SHELTER MANY
COULD AFFORD.

its topsoil at an alarming rate. The Black Blizzards are

so bad, they've been known to cover ships anchored in

the Atlantic Ocean with dust and dirt from the

southern plains.

I know the government is trying to help, but what can be done? The rest of the country is digging out of the **Great Depression** the way we're digging out of our dust storms. They've only got so much to give to help us. President Franklin D. Roosevelt has a **New Deal** plan, which is helping put some men who have lost their farms back to work. And he has also established the Soil Erosion Service and the Prairie States Forestry Project to study what led to this disaster to begin with. It would have been nice to have these agencies in place before the disaster, but all we can do is move forward. If these agencies come up with better plans for taking care of our farmlands, I'll make the changes. Since I worked on the farm as a young boy in my daddy's time, I've seen a lot of changes in farming techniques.

I'll do whatever it takes to heal and keep my land.

ABOUT 500,000 PEOPLE BECAME HOMELESS DUE
TO THE DUST BOWL AND THE DAMAGE IT CAUSED
TO THEIR HOMES AND FARMS.

2

LEONA ELLSAESSER

BLACK SUNDAY SURVIVOR

Finally, the sun is out. Until you've gone too long without the sun on your face, you have no idea how good it feels to bathe in its warmth. This is just how I felt on April 14, 1935.

We'd been stuck in the house for weeks. Dust storm after dust storm kept us prisoners in our own home. I can see why Mama and Daddy would insist we all stay inside, and they got no argument from me or my sister. The dust flew around everywhere, and you couldn't keep it out of your nose or eyes. Even going

DUST STORMS WERE ESPECIALLY DANGEROUS FOR CHILDREN. THEY WERE OFTEN KEPT HOME FROM SCHOOL OR HELD AT SCHOOL OVERNIGHT TO KEEP THEM FROM BEING OUTDOORS WHEN A DUST STORM WAS COMING.

FARMERS AND THEIR FAMILIES WHO DID VENTURE
OUTSIDE DURING A DUST STORM OFTEN WORE MASKS
TO KEEP FROM BREATHING IN SILICA PARTICLES IN THE
FLYING SOIL.

out for one minute, you'd get covered in dirt like you took a bath in the pigsty.

The dust makes people sick, too. I've heard of people getting **dust pneumonia**, which is just another way of saying your lungs get clogged with dirt. Some folks recover, but others don't.

And it's not just the people who get sick. The animals are suffering too. Daddy is a cattle dealer, and he's been losing one after another of the herd. Sometimes they check to see if it's the dust that killed an animal, and sure enough, they usually find dirt inside its lungs and belly. This is a deadly time.

No, inside is the only safe place, but even a roof and four walls doesn't always keep all the dirt out. Mama put sheets up over the windows, but it doesn't work entirely. The dirt makes little snowdrifts in the sills, except it is soil, not snow. We're constantly cleaning, but it's impossible to keep ahead of it. And the darkness is the worst! Why even the chickens don't know day from night anymore. Some of the chickens roost in the middle of the day now as if it's night!

But not today. Today is beautiful. The sun is shining, the wind is calm, and there's not a particle of dust in the air. We're all outside. Daddy is catching up on chores and my sister is enjoying the fresh air and sunshine. Mama asks if I want to go with her to the lodge. Of course, I do! I'm yearning for human company the same as I crave the sunshine. It's a beautiful Sunday. I'll bet there will be lots of folks there. Oh, it will feel good to be with other people. A trip to the lodge is just what we need. And it's not too far—just down the road in a small town called Sublette.

The visit is just what I needed to lift my lagging spirits. It's helping Mama, too. I haven't heard her laugh in weeks, but now that she's with her friends, she's like her old self again. We may have stayed a bit too long, but how could we help it? Time outside away

HOMES AND FARMS WERE DECIMATED BY THE
DECADE-LONG DROUGHT IN THE PLAINS STATES.
FOURTEEN STORMS ON THE GREAT PLAINS WERE
REPORTED IN 1932. IN 1933, THERE WERE
38 STORMS.

THE VIOLENT STORM THAT IS NOW KNOWN AS "BLACK SUNDAY" FEATURED WINDS THAT TRAVELED AS FAST AS 60 MILES (97 KM) PER HOUR. IT WAS AFTER THIS STORM THAT A REPORTER USED THE TERM "DUST BOWL" FOR THE FIRST TIME.

from home with friends—it's a rare gift. We'd be foolish not to take advantage.

Someone mentions a chill in the air. It's true. I feel it. The temperature has dropped, and so has the mood at the lodge. Any changes in the air trigger fear. Anything that might bring wind will also bring dirt and dust. Dirt and dust! It's the stuff of nightmares!

Mama's laughter is gone. She's serious now. She tells me it's time to head home. The sky is growing dark. We all know what that means. Mama says she thinks we can beat the storm if we head out now in a hurry. I follow close at her heels, and we roll the windows up tight when we get in the car. She drives faster than usual, but I don't say anything. I can see the darkness behind us in the rearview mirror. It's heading toward us at lightning speed!

Soon the car and everything around us is covered in soot and soil. The wind sounds like a freight train, and we can't even see through the windshield. Suddenly, the power shorts out in the car and everything turns off. Mama glides the car to the side of the road. She tries and tries to restart the engine, but nothing happens. The battery is dead. I know what

SECOND SOURCE

Find another source on the September 1931 duster. Compare the information there to the information here.

she's going to say, though I don't want to hear it. We're going to have to walk the rest of the way home.

It's about three-quarters of a mile (1.2 km) to our house, but I'm not sure we can make it. I cannot see a thing, not even the hand in front of my face! But I know we have no choice. We get out of the car together, but right away, we lose one another. We can't call out for each other or we'll get a mouthful of dirt. I feel around for her, but soon I am overcome with soot. The best thing for me to do is to head home. I know this road. It leads straight to our house. I just need to stay on it. Then Daddy will come get Mama, and everyone will be okay.

If Mama ever calls out for me, I don't hear it. The wind roars all around me. I cover my nose and mouth the best I can with my sleeve and squint to keep the

THE DUST BOWL AFFECTED MORE THAN 1 MILLION
ACRES (0.4 MILLION HA) OF LAND IN THE 1930S.

dirt out of my eyes. I find where the road meets the grassy edge and follow it, one step at a time. It's slow going, but I can make it. I have no choice. Mama is out in the storm. I have to rescue her. We need Daddy's help!

PLAINS HELPER

Hugh Bennett was a scientist for the U.S. Department of Agriculture. He was one of the few people who recognized the danger of plowing up the prairie. In the 1920s, he predicted a disaster—and he was right. He wrote the soil conservation practices that eventually repaired the Great Plains.

TO HELP THE SOIL HEAL, FARMERS WORKED WITH THE FEDERAL GOVERNMENT TO PLANT TREES AND GRASS IN AREAS THAT HAD ONCE GROWN CROPS IN ORDER TO MINIMIZE WIND EROSION.

SECOND SOURCE

Find another source on the conditions in the Dust Bowl. Compare the information there to the information here.

Finally, I am home! I race up the steps and into Daddy's arms. The first thing he wants to know is—where is Mama? I tell him what happened and where he'll find her. He sets off in his truck, the truck with the strong headlights. He just needs to stay on the road and he'll find her no problem. He tells me to stay with my sister. I am exhausted and filthy. He gets no argument from me.

My sister and I sit and wait . . . and wait . . . and wait. Mama's car isn't that far away, less than a mile, like I said. Daddy should have found her by now. Time moves slowly. There is no sign of Mama or Daddy. What have I done? I should never have left her alone! I should have stayed by the car until we found each other. What if she gets lost looking for me?

I go to the window out of habit, but there's no

point in trying to look out. The window is covered with a sheet, and even if it weren't, it would be too dark outside to see anything. I wouldn't dream of opening the door and letting all that dust and dirt inside. I think it's the worst storm we've ever had!

Finally, the front door bursts open. It's Daddy! He has Mama with him! She can barely catch her breath. She is covered from head to toe in soot. But she is alive and safe. I throw myself into her arms and she hugs me tight. This nightmare is over . . . for now.

3

DOROTHEA LANGE

PHOTOGRAPHER

My position is uncertain, but I believe my job is so very important. I am here with the Resettlement Administration, a government agency that is meant to help farmers through these troubled times. My official position is "clerk-stenographer," but my real purpose is to photograph what is happening in the Plains states that is driving millions of people away from what was once the most fertile farmland in the nation.

The year 1932 was difficult. It was especially hard on the folks living in the southern Plains states. Farmers in Oklahoma, Kansas—well, everywhere from Texas to Nebraska really—suffered enormously. According to reports, 273,000 families were evicted from their farms, most because they could no longer pay their bills. In October, reports showed that 34 million U.S. citizens had no income. No job at all! When Franklin D. Roosevelt was inaugurated in March 1933, he set to work right away trying to relieve the suffering by implementing an economic policy called the New Deal. It is meant to bring prosperity to places of poverty and to lift the country out of the Great Depression. I am doing my best to do my part as well.

I learned the art of photography at Columbia University and was quite happy as a portrait photographer in San Francisco. But then the Great Depression hit. I took my camera outside of my studio and captured the desperate poverty in which my fellow San Franciscans lived. Now, I feel it is my duty to travel to the southern Plains states and document these images of great misery brought on by what is known as the Dust Bowl. Though the Great Depression is a **blight** on the whole nation, it is particularly difficult for people living through the dust storms.

THINK ABOUT IT

Determine the main point of this paragraph. Pick out one piece of evidence that supports it.

For generations, farmers have been plowing the grasslands into fine soil. Now, droughts have turned the abused soil to dust, and strong winds carry that dust up into the sky, blowing it eastward. There are reports of dust storms making it all the way to New York and Washington, D.C., on the East Coast. The soil can no longer be used to grow crops. Without crops, farmers have no income.

POOR FAMILIES MOVED TOGETHER TO TRY TO FIND A
BETTER WAY OF LIFE.

It is a perfect storm of suffering. Someone must

bear witness to this suffering. That someone is me.

There is no money in the Resettlement

Administration budget for an official photographer, so

I file my film and travel expenses under "clerical
supplies." Is this ethical? I can't answer that question.
All I know is that I must have film. I must be able to
travel. There are so many stories here. I am driven to

SHANTYTOWNS, WHERE POVERTY-STRICKEN FAMILIES
LIVED IN SHACKS, WERE ALSO CALLED "HOOVERVILLES,"
AFTER PRESIDENT HERBERT HOOVER (1929-1933).

tell them all with my pictures. My husband, Paul Schuster Taylor, and I have decided to work together to share the stories of untold suffering.

It is March 1936. After six weeks of traveling through California, New Mexico, and Arizona, I decided to head home to Berkeley, California, to rest and develop my film. I drive past a sign that says "Pea-Pickers Camp." That is odd. The pea crop is frozen. There is no call for pea pickers. Who could be staying there? But I am tired and homesick. I know that I am lucky to have a home. Still, my inner voice nags me. I should turn around and investigate. What call is there for a Pea-Pickers Camp? There are no peas.

My curiosity is niggling, but not overwhelming. I drive on for 20 more miles (32 km) before my inner voice wins out. I must know what is going on at that Pea-Pickers Camp. If there is nothing there to photograph and report, I will have driven 20 miles

FLORENCE OWENS THOMPSON WAS 32 WHEN
DOROTHEA LANGE TOOK HER PICTURE IN 1936 AT A
PEA-PICKERS CAMP. THIS PICTURE MADE BOTH
THOMPSON AND LANGE FAMOUS, THOUGH THOMPSON
NEVER RECEIVED ANY MONEY FOR APPEARING IN
THE PICTURE.

(32 km) out of the way for no good reason. I press the brake and turn around. Curiosity wins.

As I pull into the muddy driveway to the camp, I come across a woman migrant worker. I am in a hurry, but she does not appear to be. She looks grim, overwhelmed, exhausted. I ask permission to take her picture and she gives it. I ask her age, and she tells me that she is 32. I do not ask her name or her history. I imagine her story is much like the others, full of hopelessness and suffering. She tells me that she and her children eat the frozen vegetables they dig up from the fields. They eat small birds that the children trap. She just sold the tires from her car to buy food.

I cannot take anymore. I return home and develop the prints. The pictures of this woman tear at my heart. I bring them to the editor of the *San*

ANALYZE THIS

Find another perspective that describes the life of migrant workers in California. How is it similar to this account? How is it different?

Francisco News. He too is taken with the suffering in her eyes, and he runs the pictures along with a story about starving migrant workers. The story prompts the federal government to deliver 20,000 pounds (9,000 kilograms) of food to starving workers, but by that time, this woman and her children have moved on.

I name the picture *Migrant Mother*. Though I have a comfortable home with my husband, it is this

THE GRAPES OF WRATH

John Steinbeck's 1939 novel *The Grapes of Wrath* depicts the plight of Dust Bowl migrants through the story of the fictional Joad family. The Joads trek from Oklahoma to California, suffering scorn and hardship as they seek honest work. It is still widely read and discussed.

woman who compels me to return day after day, week after week, year after year with my camera to document the human suffering.

In California, I see a little girl. She is standing on the side of the road holding a long sack. I wonder if it is bigger than she is. The little girl stands there squinting and trying to keep the sun out of her eyes while I snap my pictures. It is only 7 o'clock in the morning. I wonder if the little girl has eaten breakfast. I wonder if she will eat at all today. She certainly cannot eat the cotton it is her job to pick. My heart breaks for her plight.

I am as moved by their resilience as I am by their suffering. People who have lost everything—their land, their homes, and in some cases, the lives of their loved ones—take the time to plant trees and flowers. Shantytowns called "Okievilles" in California, built by Oklahomans who have fled their homesteads, are merely flimsy shacks where no human should have to live. Yet these homes "represent many a last stand to self-respect," I write in my notes.

I photograph a family from Oklahoma on a highway between Blythe and Indio, California. They abandoned their drought-stricken farm and drove as far as they could toward California. Their car broke down within a day's journey to their destination—Bakersfield—and they abandoned the car and whatever possessions they could not carry.

I photograph four families, all related, with 15 children between them, living in a single tent in California. It is all they can afford. Many live in homes that are not fit for human habitation. "They have built homes here out of nothing," I write in my notes. Some are built of plywood and cardboard. The people are hopeless. "Somethin' is radical wrong," one tells me. "I don't believe the president knows what is happening to us here," says another.

I photograph a family walking on the highway.

MIGRANT WORKER CAMPS WERE FILLED WITH HOMEMADE SHELTERS USING TENTS, TARPS, AND CARDBOARD.

There are five children. They began their journey in Idabel, Oklahoma, and are headed toward Krebs, Oklahoma, in Pittsburg County. The father lost their farm when he became sick with pneumonia. He cannot find work and he has no income.

Of all the photographs I have taken, it is the *Migrant Mother* that I will never forget. She is the nameless face of misery in the Dust Bowl.

TIMELINE

THE DUST BOWL

The Homestead Act provides settlers with 160 acres (65 ha) of land.

1862

The Kinkaid Act expands the ability to obtain free public land.

1904

The Enlarged Homestead Act leads to a larger influx of inexperienced farmers in the southern Plains states.

1909

1910S & 1920S

World War I increases Europe's demand for wheat. Farms in the Plains states struggle to keep up and tear up grasslands to make room for more farmland.

1931

A nearly decade-long drought begins. Crops begin to fail. Eroding soil leads to devastating dust storms.

1935

The term "Dust Bowl" is used for the first time after Black Sunday, April 14.

1941

Average rains return, essentially ending the Dust Bowl conditions.

Take a close look at this photograph of the Black Blizzard and answer the following questions:

1. What would a farmer see in this picture? What would concern the farmer? What would happen to the farmer's family, home, and livelihood if this type of storm kept coming again and again?

2. What would the child of a farmer see in this picture? What would he or she think of clouds of dust enveloping homes and farms? Would he or she feel in danger? Why?

3. What would a photographer whose job it was to document the terrible weather conditions see in this picture? What would the photographer want others to know about the Dust Bowl? Does the picture show the dangers of living in the Plains states during the Dust Bowl? How?

GLOSSARY

Black Blizzards *(BLACK BLIZZ-erdz)* particularly strong and brutal dust storms

blight *(BLAIT)* something that causes other things to be in a deteriorated condition

brink *(BRINGK)* an edge or threshold where something unpleasant is about to happen

Dust Bowl *(DUST BOHL)* an area in the Great Plains of the United States destroyed by erosion and wind storms during the 1930s

dust pneumonia *(DUST noo-MOAN-yuh)* a respiratory sickness that happens when the lungs fill with dust

furrow *(FUR-oh)* a small groove or trench made with a plow

Great Depression *(GRATE dih-PRESH-un)* a long and severe recession in the U.S. economy during the late 1920s and 1930s

livestock *(LAIV-stahk)* farm animals

mechanism *(MEK-a-niz-um)* a system of parts that work together in a machine

New Deal *(NOO DEEL)* economic programs sponsored by the U.S. government during the 1930s that were designed to make the economy stronger and bring the country out of the Great Depression

profit *(PRAH-fit)* financial gain

LEARN MORE

FURTHER READING

Blake, Kevin. *Sick Soil: The Dust Bowl.* New York: Bearport Publishing, 2018.

Rea, Amy C. *Perspectives on the Dust Bowl.* Mankato, MN: 12-Story Library, 2018.

Vander Zee, Ruth. *Next Year: Hope in the Dust.* Mankato, MN: Creative Education, 2017.

WEBSITES

The Dust Bowl
https://www.history.com/topics/dust-bowl
This website describes what caused the Dust Bowl and what happened during the Black Blizzards.

Living History
https://livinghistoryfarm.org/
farminginthe30s/water_02.html
This website explains what life was like for farmers and their families who lived through the Dust Bowl.

INDEX

ABOUT THE AUTHOR

Kristin J. Russo is a university English lecturer. She loves teaching, reading, writing, and learning new things. She and her husband live near Providence, Rhode Island, in a small house surrounded by flower gardens. They have three grown children and three rescue dogs.